ME TOO!® BOOKS

BIG ENEMY, BIGGER GOD!

THE STORY OF GIDEON

By Marilyn Lashbrook

Illustrated by Stephanie McFetridge Britt

RAINBOW
STUDIES
INTERNATIONAL

El Reno, Oklahoma

Creating Colorful Treasures™

ME TOO! ® Books are designed to help you
share the joy of reading with children. They
provide a new and fun way to improve a
child's reading skills — by practice and
example. At the same time, you are teaching
your children valuable Bible truths.

BIG ENEMY, BIGGER GOD! is an exciting
and fast-moving story that will provide
plenty of opportunities for children to read
with expression. This book will also help
children to understand the importance of
remembering to put God first in their lives.
It will reassure them that God forgives us
when we forget and helps us to fight our
battles against the enemy.

Reading is the key to successful education.
Obeying the principles of God's Word
opens the door to a successful life.
ME TOO! ® Books encourage your
children in both!

Bold type:	Child reads.
Regular type:	Adult reads.

 Wait for child to respond.

 Talk about it!

Library of Congress Catalog Card Number: 98-065501
ISBN 0-933657-89-7

Art direction and design by Chris Schechner Graphic Design.
Production and film by Paragon Communications Group, Inc.

1 2 3 4 5 6 7 8 9 — 02 01 00 99 98
Rainbow Studies International, El Reno, OK 73036, U.S.A.

BIG ENEMY, BIGGER GOD!

THE STORY OF GIDEON

Taken from Judges 6 and 7

When would God's people learn?

First, they sinned against God.

Second, their enemies bullied them.

Third, they cried out to God for help.

Fourth, God saved them.

Fifth, they forgot God.

Then the people sinned. The whole story started all over again . . . and again . . . and again . . . and again!

This time the Israelites were in real trouble. For seven years their enemies had tormented them. For seven years they continued to worship idols. They didn't learn very quickly!

God's people were living in caves. They were starving. They were hiding from their enemies.

One big army came after them. Next, a bigger army came after them. Then all the armies of the East came after them.

Can you imagine trying to count all the grains of sand on the beach? That's what it would have been like to count the enemy soldiers. Impossible! There were too many to count.

God's people were ready to pray! They cried out to the Lord to save them and He heard their cry. God sent someone to help.

Gideon was chosen to lead the army of Israel. God promised to be with him.

Gideon gathered an army. He had only 32,000 men. That was not a very big army to fight so many enemies.

God spoke to Gideon. "Your army is too big!"

Too big! How could it be too big?

God did not want His people to brag. He wanted them to know they could not win by themselves. With a small army, they would have to trust God.

Gideon obeyed God. He said to his men, "Anyone who is afraid may leave."

Suddenly his army was much smaller. All but 10,000 men went home.

Gideon's army was now very small. How could he fight an army that was too big to count?

But Gideon was in for another surprise. God spoke again. He said, "Your army is still too big!"

Too big! How could his army be too big?

Gideon didn't understand. He didn't think his army was too big. But he obeyed God. Have you ever had to obey a rule you didn't understand? What was the rule? Why should you obey your parents even when you don't want to? ⬣

Gideon trusted God. He believed God knew best. Gideon took the men to the river. He separated the men who lapped water in

their hands from those who put their faces in the river.

Slurp! Slurp!

Gideon sent 9,700 men home. Now he had only 300 men. What could 300 men do against such a big army? Nothing, without God's help. But with God's help they would win.

That night God told Gideon to go to battle. "If you are afraid, go down to the enemy camp with your servant. Listen to what they have to say."

Gideon was afraid. Who wouldn't be afraid to fight with only 300 men?

So Gideon and his servant sneaked down to the edge of the enemy camp. They tiptoed close enough to overhear two soldiers talking.

"I had a dream," one man said. "It was a silly dream. A loaf of bread bounced into our camp and knocked over a tent. Can you imagine that?"

The other man said, "Your dream meant that God has given our camp to Gideon."

When Gideon heard that, he could hardly keep from jumping and shouting. He quietly worshiped the Lord, then he hurried back to his little army.

It didn't matter if he had three men, three hundred men or three million men. God promised he would win, and God would keep His promise.

When Gideon arrived back at his own camp, he commanded, "Get up! The Lord has given the enemy into our hands."

Gideon divided his men into three groups. Each man carried a sword, a trumpet and a torch. Each torch was covered by a pitcher.

"Watch me," Gideon said. "Do what I do."

Gideon and his men went in different directions. They crept through the darkness and silently surrounded the great snoring army.

Gideon blew his trumpet and broke his pitcher. His torch shone in the darkness.

Then his men did the same thing. They blew three hundred trumpets. They broke three hundred pitchers. They held up three hundred torches. They shouted, "A sword for the Lord and for Gideon!"

Their enemies woke up when they heard the noise. They stumbled from their tents. They were terrified.

God caused Israel's enemies to fight each other. In the darkness they did not know they were fighting their own men. Many were killed. Some ran, but the people of God captured them.

God gave Gideon and his little army a great big victory. The people of God were safe at last.

Soon the people came to Gideon. "Rule over us," they begged. "You saved us."

What? Gideon did not save them. He just followed orders. God had saved them!

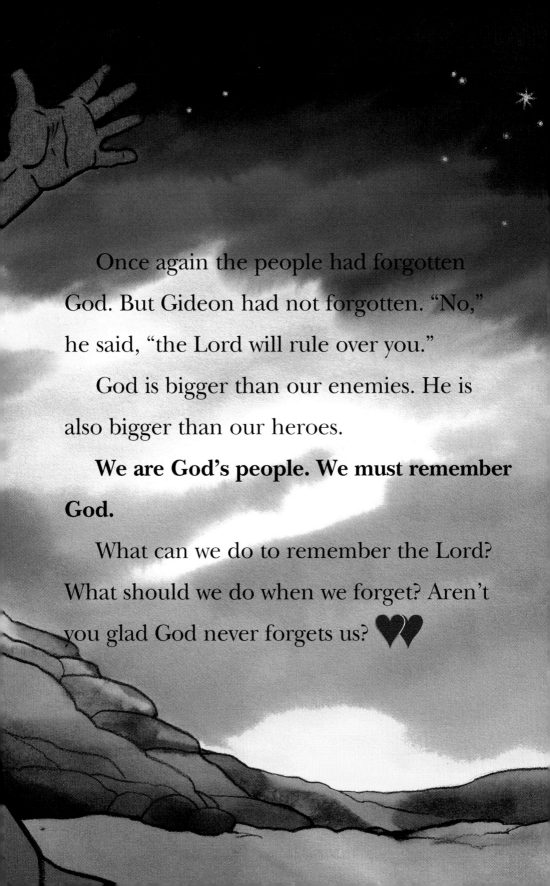

Once again the people had forgotten God. But Gideon had not forgotten. "No," he said, "the Lord will rule over you."

God is bigger than our enemies. He is also bigger than our heroes.

We are God's people. We must remember God.

What can we do to remember the Lord? What should we do when we forget? Aren't you glad God never forgets us?

ME TOO!®
B O O K S

Ages 2-7

SOMEONE TO LOVE THE STORY OF CREATION	**NO TREE FOR CHRISTMAS** THE STORY OF JESUS' BIRTH
TWO BY TWO THE STORY OF NOAH'S FAITH	**NOW I SEE** THE STORY OF THE MAN BORN BLIND
I DON'T WANT TO THE STORY OF JONAH	**DON'T ROCK THE BOAT!** THE STORY OF THE MIRACULOUS CATCH
I MAY BE LITTLE THE STORY OF DAVID'S GROWTH	**OUT ON A LIMB** THE STORY OF ZACCHAEUS
I'LL PRAY ANYWAY THE STORY OF DANIEL	**SOWING AND GROWING** THE PARABLE OF THE SOWER AND THE SOILS
WHO NEEDS A BOAT? THE STORY OF MOSES	**DON'T STOP. . . FILL EVERY POT** THE STORY OF THE WIDOW'S OIL
GET LOST, LITTLE BROTHER THE STORY OF JOSEPH	**GOOD, BETTER, BEST** THE STORY OF MARY AND MARTHA
THE WALL THAT DID NOT FALL THE STORY OF RAHAB'S FAITH	**GOD'S HAPPY HELPERS** THE STORY OF TABITHA AND FRIENDS

Ages 5-10

IT'S NOT MY FAULT MAN'S BIG MISTAKE	**NOTHING TO FEAR** JESUS WALKS ON WATER	**NOBODY KNEW BUT GOD** MIRIAM AND BABY MOSES
GOD, PLEASE SEND FIRE! ELIJAH AND THE PROPHETS OF BAAL	**THE BEST DAY EVER** THE STORY OF JESUS	**MORE THAN BEAUTIFUL** THE STORY OF ESTHER
TOO BAD, AHAB NABOTH'S VINEYARD	**THE GREAT SHAKE-UP** MIRACLES IN PHILIPPI	**FAITH TO FIGHT** THE STORY OF CALEB
THE WEAK STRONGMAN SAMSON	**TWO LADS AND A DAD** THE PRODIGAL SON	**BIG ENEMY, BIGGER GOD** THE STORY OF GIDEON

WE SEE!™
V I D E O S

VIDEOS FOR TODAY'S CHRISTIAN FAMILY.
51 animated Bible stories from the Old Testament ("In the Beginning" Series) and New Testament ("A Kingdom without Fron-
tiers" Series) will provide your children with a solid cornerstone of spiritual support.

Available at your local bookstore or from:

Rainbow Studies International
P.O. Box 759 • El Reno, Oklahoma 73036 • 1-800-242-5348

RSI
Creating Colorful Treasures™